Wild Animals Need Help

By Roberta Smithson

Scott Foresman
is an imprint of

Glenview, Illinois • Boston, Massachusetts • Mesa, Arizona
Shoreview, Minnesota • Upper Saddle River, New Jersey

Photographs
Every effort has been made to secure permission and provide appropriate credit for photographic material. The publisher deeply regrets any omission and pledges to correct errors called to its attention in subsequent editions.

Unless otherwise acknowledged, all photographs are the property of Pearson Education, Inc.

3 ©Pete Atkinson/Jupiter Images; 4 ©Eric Gevaert/Shutterstock; 5 ©David Hosking/Corbis; 6 ©Georgette Douwma/Getty Images; 7 Jupiter Images; 8 ©George Grall/Getty Images

ISBN 13: 978-0-328-39738-9
ISBN 10:   0-328-39738-5

2 3 4 5 6 7 8 9 10 V059 17 16 15 14 13 12 11 10 09

Whales need help.

Apes need help.

Birds need help.

Turtles need help.

Tigers need help.

Butterflies need help.